$100 Millions in IRA

Rochit Rajsuman

Comments and questions on this book can be sent at
zerotax@justifyworld.com

$100 Millions In IRA

Rochit Rajsuman, Ph. D.

JustifyWorld Inc.

Library of Congress Cataloging-in-Publication Data
Rajsuman, Rochit
$100 Millions in IRA / Rochit Rajsuman
ISBN 978-09857370-1-6 (Kindle)
ISBN 978-14783157-1-1 (Paperback)
1. Politics 2. Mitt Romney 3. Presidential Candidate
4. Taxes 5. Presidential Election
I. Title

© **2012 JustifyWorld Inc.**

International Standard Book Number 978-09857370-1-6
 978-14783157-1-1 (Paperback)

10 9 8 7 6 5 4 3 2 1

$100 Millions In IRA

Table of Contents

Disclaimer

This book contains political commentary and speculative scenarios. JustifyWorld Inc. and author take no responsibility for any or all scenarios given in this book, they may or may not match with the reality.

The book also contains suggestions on life style choices. JustifyWorld Inc. and author take no responsibility of any damages to anyone if someone tries to implement any suggestion given in this book. These life-style choices are given in generalized form and do not consider specific details. Person considering such choices should first consult with his/her attorney, accountant and other relevant professionals, and check local, state and federal laws before taking any action.

Preface

Whole America is in shock to learn the size of Individual Retirement Account (IRA) of the Republican Presidential candidate Mitt Romney. Some experts have estimated the value of his IRA over $100 Millions.

Pundits are scratching their head, how can it be? Isn't there a contribution limit? How can one amass $100 millions in the retirement account? Did Mitt Romney violate laws? Why didn't IRS check? Is it another case of regulators sleeping on the job?

Along with the tax debate, from media reports, it appears to me that people would probably be not so shocked if money was in a taxable account. But because the money is in an IRA, people want to know how it was done. If it was done legally than they can also use the same method and shelter their assets.

In my previous book, "In Your Face IRS: Zero Taxes", I mentioned that I was pissed and subsequently started to look into finances, tax laws and possible scenarios one can use. Finances of Mitt Romney have drawn so much attention that I could not resist thinking about it. It may be fun to poke at him but I also see it as a great and unprecedented opportunity to learn. People complain that they are paying too much in taxes; well, learn from him and use the same methods, who is stopping?

The highlights of Mitt Romney's 2010 tax return are: Adjusted Gross Income (AGI) of $21,646,507; this includes $3,327,678 of qualified dividends (15% tax rate); he took $4,519,140 in deductions, reducing taxable income to $17,120,067. Taxes on this $17M being $2,873,054; with $232,989 in Alternative Minimum Tax (AMT) minus $129,697 in foreign tax credits, net taxes being $2,976,345. He further added self employment tax and credit for social security taxes paid for household help, making his 2010 taxes as $3,009,766 (13.9% of AGI of $21.6M).

The income in long-term capital gains, $3.3M in dividends and deductions of $4.5M is what made his tax rate to drop. Set aside the politics for a moment, whatever he did to have such large deduction, it worked well with the IRS, a lesson to be learned.

There is even a bigger lesson than deductions – he didn't created much in the ordinary income that is taxed at higher rate; and that amount is also very well structured.

Hence, I think the whole tax return is very good example for all of us to learn how to structure ordinary income, how to take deductions and reduce taxable income. If we (common people) don't learn and don't take allowable deductions, it is our fault; nobody is stopping us. If we learn the basics, we might be able to extend it!

In terms of his IRA, we have only bits and pieces of information, but it is worth while to examine them. Examination also allows to imagine and speculate on how someone can accumulate $100 millions or even Billion in an IRA.

Initially, I didn't want to write this book; what I have learned and what I can imagine; it would only educate other rich people, some of them may not know how to stash away hundreds of millions.

It is likely that some people will call it a political book. Hence, I want to make it clear that I don't have any political agenda. I am not affiliated with any party, never have been. Frankly, the way leaders of both parties including elected members of the congress have been behaving lately, I will be very happy if both parties are voted out and ET takes over.

In the absence of ET, solution might be to outsource legislative jobs – it will save tons of money for the United States Corporation. But the President wants to keep jobs here. Can someone convince him that outsourcing of the Congress is necessary to cut expenses; it is good for the corporation and shareholders, the public.

In "In Your Face IRS: Zero Taxes", I in-fact suggested to vote for independent candidates rather than Republicans or Democrats.

Hence, I had a second dilemma – Should I write something that would be viewed as political, in this case anti-Republicans?

The basic question I was facing, should I stay put and keep quite? That didn't sound right either – public should know and learn just like I am learning.

I came to a compromise – I will sketch-out the most likely scenario; I will also sketch-out a better scenario that Mitt Romney could have used but certainly didn't; and as a compromise, I will sketch-out some of the lessons we (the common folks) can learn.

In terms of poking fun, my compromise is to restrain myself to a sentence here and a sentence there. I will just indicate certain items that readers themselves may want to poke around but I will myself not go into details.

Two more comments before I get to the meat:

1. My English was poor to begin with and I always had something more important to do than spend time to improve my English. I am not writing a novel. In scientific papers and books, my focus was scientific concept, circuits, equation/formula etc. In a book such as this, my focus is on business/tax concepts. English grammar is not even secondary priority for me. It's a fair warning that you will encounter numerous grammatical and syntactical errors while reading this book.

2. I am a scientist/engineer by education and past work. I turned away from science and engineering when I was pissed-off in 2010 after Treasury shoved over Trillion dollars to banks in the name of should've, would've, could've. I am still in the learning phase but I have found reading numbers in

accounting, taxation, finance etc. is very simple and easy – it is elementary Arithmetic. Once in a while, a tiny bit of Statistics when there is a projection, but that's about it.

Engineers connect various pieces to make something; apparently it can also be done in business finances, accounting etc. I find it easy to sketch-out various models Wall-Streeters have used, even models that they haven't think-of yet and can use.

For example, while regulators are not thinking and taking precautionary steps, I can envision banks bundling student loans and sell credit swaps just like they did with home mortgage based derivatives. More than a Trillion dollars in student loans are sitting collecting dust. Student loans are unforgivable; hence, credit agencies will have no problem in giving AAA ratings. Lives of millions of students could be bought and sold, but nothing illegal!

Another example, Mitt Romney's IRA is tax deferred money. I can think-of ways how he could have made it tax exempt; he still can, all of it, without violating any laws. He didn't make laws; congress did. He can simply follow laws. I will write little bit more on it later in the text.

I am just an average engineer/scientist; the world is full of brilliant scientists. My worry is if some of them are pissed-off because of the way lawmakers and government officials are behaving, they will create scenarios that Wall-Street banker can't even dream-of in their wildest dream. And these scenarios will be perfectly within the laws, unlike wall-street practices of insider trading, cooking books, running Ponzi schemes, fixing LIBOR interest rate or even flat-out gambling/hedging.

Because of the educational system in the country and the "fear of mathematics", numbers that seem complicated and complex to some people are simple and almost child's play to most engineers and scientists, reading numbers is in their blood. If their minds turned towards finances, the scenario they will create will not be limited to simple Arithmetic and Statistics. To create derivative financial instruments, they will use real Differential Calculus, Divergence and Curl of directional field (Vector Calculus), after-all money, economy, taxes are all vectors; mapping is easy.

Don't worry, I won't write equations in this book. I also won't write my puny scenarios that Wall-Street can use. But my point will become clear when you read the scenario I have written for Mitt Romney that he didn't use, but could have to get tax exempt status for the money in his IRA rather simply deferring it until withdrawn.

But I think that the value readers will find by reading this book is description on things I have learned by examining his tax return – what we commoners can do and how.

Chapter 1: Introduction: The Facts

Let me start with known facts. Regardless of how much hoopla is in the media, the fact is that nobody knows the real value of Mitt Romney's IRA (except of-course Mitt Romney and other handful of people such as his CPA). Some people have extrapolated numbers and suggested a value of his IRA in the range of $21 millions to $102 millions. People also seem unable to imagine how one can amass a large sum such as $100 millions in IRA. In media reports, I have seen statements from pundits explaining up to a possibility of about $10 millions but no further.

$100 millions has nice ring to it; hence, in rest of the book, I will use the word $100 millions.

In terms of tax return, he has disclosed 2010 return that includes:

1. Form 1040 and supplemental documents

2. 1041 return of Mitt Romney Blind Trust

3. 1041 return of Ann Romney Blind Trust

4. 1041 of Ann and Mitt Romney Family Trust.

5. 990-PF return of Tyler Charitable Foundation

These documents are available on his web-site. The web-site also has Request for extension and 2011 estimates. Any number in an estimate has no real meaning; these numbers may be exactly same as actual numbers or miles away from the actual numbers. Hence, I didn't bother to look at them.

In 2010 return, following documents are included:

1. Form 1040
2. Schedule A, itemized deductions
3. Schedule B, interest and ordinary dividends
4. Schedule C, profit and loss from business for author/speaking fees.
5. Schedule C, profit and loss from business for director's fees; $113,881 cash, from Marriott International.

6. Schedule D, capital gain and losses; with and without AMT

7. Schedule E, supplemental income and loss

8. Schedule SE, self employment tax

9. Form 1116, foreign tax credit: passive category and general category; with and without AMT

10. Form 3800, general business credit

11. Form 4797, sales of business property; with and without AMT

12. Form 6251, alternative minimum tax – individuals

13. Schedule H, household employment tax

14. Form 4952, investment interest expense deduction; with and without AMT

15. Form 4562, depreciation and amortization

16. Form 8621, return by a shareholder of a passive foreign investment company. A number of copies of this form have been used for various companies. Because the location of these companies has become a political issue, I will list them later.

17. Form 5884, work opportunity credit

18. Form 6252, installment sale income

19. Form 6781, gains and losses from section 1256 contracts and straddles

20. Form 8582, passive activity loss limitations; with and without AMT

21. Form 8582-CR, passive activity credit limitations

22. Form 8846, credit for employer social security and medicare taxes paid

23. Form 8865, return of US persons with respect to certain foreign partnerships

24. Schedule O, transfer of property to a foreign partnership

25. Form 5471, information return of US persons with respect to certain foreign corporations

26. Schedule J, accumulated earning and profits of controlled foreign corporation

27. Schedule M, transactions between controlled foreign corporation and shareholders

28. Form 926, return by a US transferor of property to a foreign corporation. Two copies

of the form have been used to identify various companies in Ireland; transferee is listed as Goldman Sachs; amount being $1,523,419 and $139,625.

29. Form 8886, reportable transaction disclosure statement. Multiple copies have been used for family trust and Ann Romney Blind trust; associated summary letters from Goldman Sachs Hedge Fund Partners, LLC, and Brookside Capital Partners Fund list number of companies and foreign currency transactions.

30. Form 8903, domestic production activities deduction. Domestic production gross receipts are listed at $32,236; allocable cost of good sold being $22,262.

31. Form 8283, noncash charitable contribution. A total of 95,284 shares of an un-named company to Tyler Foundation at fair market value of $1,458,807.

32. Form 8948, preparer explanation for not filing electronically.

33. Letters of 83(b) election for Bain Capital. Letters are dated Oct. 22, 2010; date of property transfer is also listed as Oct. 22, 2010.

34. 69 statement pages, these are explanations and details for various forms.

On Form 1040, his Adjusted Gross Income (AGI) is listed as $21,646,507 (on Form 8903, line11, taxable income without domestic production activity is listed as $21,646,768; domestic production activity being ABT Solamere Founders Fund); itemized deductions $4,519,140 ($3,672,141 in 2009), making taxable income $17,120,067. The sum of all payments and tax credits (foreign tax credit) is listed as $4,619,207; tax liability $3,009,766; hence, he received a refund of $1,609,441.

On schedule A, main itemized deductions are:

I. State and local income taxes and real estate taxes are $898,946 ($749,547 in 2009).

II. Investment interest expenses $51,444

III. Gift to charity $2,983,974 (one charity being Tyler Charitable Foundation non-cash contribution of $1,458,807; other charity being Church of Latter-day Saints, cash contribution of $1,525,167).

IV. Other expenses, miscellaneous deductions $1,017,706. From statement 6, it is contribution to Partnerships, S Corporation and Estate and Trust. This is one of the items, people will enjoy dissecting; it certainly contains a learning lesson for me that I will mention in the next chapter. After subtracting 2% of AGI, the amount became $584,776.

In schedule D, little more than $17M in capital gains are listed; majority of it came from (i) Ann and Mitt Romney Family Trust; (ii) Mitt Romney Blind Trust; (iii) and Ann Romney Blind Trust. A small portion came from ABT Solamere Founders Fund and Mitt Romney 1996 CRUT.

The biggest adjustment is carryover loss of $4,844,089; the net long term capital gain is listed as $12,118,710. Net short term gain is listed as $454,539.

In schedule SE, for self employment tax, $593,996 is listed as net profit; the tax being $29,151 and deduction for one-half of self employment tax $14,576[1].

On Form 1116, Foreign Tax Credits are given:

1. In Passive category income, line 1a gross income of $1,525,982; line 3e Gross income from all sources $27,283,915; line 3a itemized deductions $1,483,722; line 2 expenses $983,944. Alternative Minimum Tax version lists line 1a $1,751,955; line 2 $983,944; line 3a none; and line 3e $26,763,809.

2. Form 1116, general category income, line 2 expenses are $17,292; line 3a itemized deduction $1,398,298. Line 3e gross income of all sources

---

[1] If only one person is self-employed, tax should be half.

$27,283,915. Alternate Minimum Tax version lists line 1a none; line 2 $17,292; line 3b other deductions $14,576; line 3e $26,763,809.

On form 3800, General Business Credit, net income tax is listed as $2,976,346.

On schedule H, Household Employment Taxes; statement 49 has details. Total social security taxes for four employees are listed as $20,603; employer being Ann Romney:

Employee	Social Security / Medicare Tax	FUTA Tax	Fed Income Tax Withheld
Rosania Costa	$4808	$4808	None
Kelli Harrison	$8667	$7000	$737
Susan Moore	$2238	$2238	$230
Valerie Cravens Anae	$4890	$4890	None

The sum of Fed Income Tax Withheld is $967.

On form 8582, $2,274,956 are listed as passive activity loss. With Alternate Minimum Tax, the amount is $2,215,267.

On Form 8621, pro-rate share of the ordinary income of $10,177 is listed from Bain Capital (ST), Luxembourg SARL. Similarly, $12,381 is listed from URSA Funding, Luxembourg.

On Form 8865, for Golden Gate Opportunity Fund, Cayman Islands, nonrecourse liability of $11,956 is listed. On schedule O for Ann Romney Blind Trust, $172,109 is listed as transfer of property to a foreign partnership for the Golden Gate Opportunity Fund.

Form 5471 discloses 12,000 common shares of Sankaty High Yield Asset Investors Ltd., Bermuda.

On Form 8886, Ann Romney Blind Trust is listed as a partner for Brookside Capital Partners Fund II LP, with reportable transaction as foreign currency transaction.

Any violations of the law

May be, may be not. But before I discuss that I couldn't help noticing certain things for fun:

a. No tax preparation fee is listed. The tax return was prepared by Daniel Feheley of Price Waterhouse Coopers LLP. May be I don't need to pay $40-$50 to buy H&R Block's TaxCut if Price Waterhouse Coopers can prepare my taxes for free.

b. No car(s) licensing renewal fees. On schedule A, itemized deductions, and on statement 5, $146 are listed as personal property taxes. Is that it? I have old cars and pay about $216, is California ripping me off?

c. Because of the health care debate, people may want to know how much was his health care insurance? On schedule A and on statement 5, $14,176 is listed as self employed health insurance premiums.

d. Warren Buffet says his secretary pays higher tax rate than him; well, seems like so is Mitt Romney's household help.

e. Being unemployed is a better choice than being self-employed. Your investment income may be in millions but you need not to pay FICA taxes when you are unemployed.

Before I get to other fun items, I noted that the R. Bradford Malt, Ropes and Gray LLP, Prudential Tower, Boston is listed as Trustee on three Trusts. The name of Mitt Romney is not listed. Hence, you can say that these returns are irrelevant; indeed, he has mentioned that there is a trustee who is in-charge.

But then, why giving us irrelevant documents; instead, he should release Form 1120 of large number of his companies for which he was in-charge, i.e. director/CEO (little bit more on it later).

The address on the return of Tyler Foundation is c/o R. Bradford Malt, Boston; people/businesses use c/o address to direct mail to an address that is convenient for them.

In terms of violation of tax laws, when Tax Return became a political issue in the Primary, only 2010 return was released. It is safe to assume that all large numbers were checked and re-checked before the release, when numbers checked-out, tax return was released.

As happens in the murder mysteries, big events don't hold the clue; it is the little things. On various large numbers, people can marvel how it was done but they won't find anything wrong; all large numbers will check out fine.

But fun items, certainly, that's what politicians for.

My objective was to learn and indeed I learned few things, some of them I will mention in the next chapter. But for readers interested in fun, let me list one example and indicate few other items that readers can poke around themselves to have fun.

I have learned a basic principle – if you want fun, look at small things; in this case, numbers that are in thousands or hundreds. Few thousand dollars are not small for most people, but they are relatively small in the context of millions:

Example: According to Schedule H and Statement 49, amount of $20,603 was paid as social security/medicare taxes for four employees. Schedule H and Form 1040, line 59 includes the credit of $4,270.

Schedule H and statement 49 also identify that no Federal Income Taxes were withheld for two employees and only $737 and $230 were withheld for other two; no state taxes were withheld. The Social Security Taxes for these two were $8667 and $2238 respectively.

SS taxes of $8667 represent a fairly good salary but withholding only $737 is a likely violation of the law. Similarly, not withholding any Federal Income Tax for Rosania Costa and Valerie Cravens Anae is also a likely violation of the law; they also had fairly good salary, three of them had salary better than average American salary of $40,000 a year.

If I extrapolate numbers, even for Susan Moore, much more money should have been withheld rather than just $230, no matter how many exemptions are listed on W-2.

Tax withholding is a responsibility of the employer – withheld a certain amount for Federal and State income taxes. Did Ann Romney was not following employment laws while she hired 4 people?

But you know, at least she was paying them well, including unemployment insurance. In California, we don't even know the household help if we find problem in their immigration status.

More Items Readers May Poke For Fun

1) One of my neighbors had a bulldog, having a Family Bulldog is fun. They lie around lazily until someone poke at them. Readers may want to poke the Family Bulldog, it would be fun.

2) While talking about laziness, readers definitely may want to poke and wake it up, if something has been lazing around for 40-years.

3) We are indeed a nation of very generous people; Tyler Foundation gave away $1,926,000 for the year 2008 – table in Part V of Foundation's return.

4) According to statement 30, in 1040, amount of $81,461 was paid as foreign taxes in 2009 but none of it was used as foreign tax credit; it was carryover to 2010. On statement 31, $62,524 was used as foreign tax credit in

2009 and subsequently $18,937 was carried over to 2011. The AMT version of statement 35, $71,069 was used as foreign tax credit in 2009 and leftover $10,392 was carryover to 2010. My math got all messed-up in time travel; this is why I need to learn.

5) Form 1116 specifies that foreign taxes were paid on 12/31/10. Trust returns also specify foreign taxes were paid on 12/31/10. I was glad to see someone was working on Friday, even if it was New Year's Eve; I am just a bit confused on who received these payments in various foreign countries that have holiday on the New Year's Eve.

6) Various BC business entities located in Luxemburg as well as URSA Funding, Luxemburg were disposed. I couldn't find the sale price and cost basis values, if readers can find it, please let me know. Don't expect IRS asking any questions; government official work hard and sleep a lot.

7) The letters to IRS, identifying section 83(b) election for various properties including BC is dated Oct. 22, 2010. The date of property transfer is also given as Oct. 22, 2010. I think it was Saturday. I understand after-hour trading and I have to respect people working on Saturdays.

8) Form 1040, line 17, income from rental real estate, royalties, partnerships, S corporations, trusts etc. is listed as -$279,884. Readers may want to double check that it was negative income and not a loss and learn; I did.

9) Schedule C, profit and loss from business (sole proprietorship), lists principal business as independent artists, writers, performers; business name as author/speaking fees. It also lists advertising expenses of $9000; and commissions and fees $39,756. Readers should make a note – when someone invites to give a speech, reconfirm who will pay.

10) On statement 22, supplement to schedule E, amount of $29,282 is listed as self-charged interest for the Family Trust; the same is true for statement 23, for Ann Romney Blind trust. Who got that income? I also need to figure it out what interest rate I should be charging from me.

11) Statement 24 lists an amount of $60,499 as swap income loss for Ann Romney Blind trust.

Some fun items have already become political issues. Let me also list what is already been reported in media:

1. A number of foreign investment companies are listed:

   a. Centro Properties Group, Victoria, AS

   b. Swiss Prime Site-Reg, Olten, SZ.

   c. Bain Capital, Luxembourg[2]

---

[2] A large number of business entities are listed. I will discuss it in Chapter 2.

d. URSA Funding, Luxembourg

e. CGS Credit Opportunities, SARL

f. CGS Collateral Manager SPV Ltd.

g. Castle Garden Funding, George Town, Cayman Islands

h. Babson 2006-1, George Town, Cayman Islands

i. Golden Gate Capital Opportunity Fund, Cayman Islands.

j. Sankaty High Yield Asset Investors Ltd, Bermuda.

k. Investments are also listed in BNY Fund of Ireland via Goldman Sachs; in Barracuda Investments Ltd, Ireland; and in Guild House via Goldman Sachs. Fair market value of transfer of property (Form 926) is listed as cash $1,523,419. Similarly, cash $139,625 is listed as property transfer to Matsack Trust Ltd., Ireland.

2. The letters to IRS, identifying section 83(b) election for Partnership Interest in Bain Capital is

dated Oct. 22, 2010. The letter is a legal document establishes partnership until Oct. 21, 2010.

3. 2009 amnesty of foreign account holders has been mentioned by a number of people as a possible reason why 2009 or earlier tax returns were not disclosed.

4. Ownership of shares of foreign car maker Toyota Motor from Dec-08 is listed. For those who might have forgotten, Mitt Romney called for bankruptcy and Chapter 11 restructuring for American car makers such as General Motors.

5. Ownership of shares of Chinese companies is listed. These include China Life Insurance Co Ltd from April-08, Hang Lung PPTYS Ltd ADR from Dec-08.

6. Ownership of shares of Indian company Infosys Technologies ADR is listed from March-09. For those who may not know, Infosys has a very large pool of tech workers; many people call it

outsourcing business. A number of US companies have laid-off workers in US and gave contracts to company such as Infosys to do the same tasks.

A number of people have been asking for disclosure of 2009 and earlier tax returns. I can't understand why no one is asking the full disclosure for 2010 that Mitt Romney has agreed to. Five tax returns that have been disclosed are hardly a fraction; probably not even 10% of his 2010 tax information.

When a person is sole everything (sole director, sole shareholder, sole executive) of a company, company's tax returns are equally relevant. I can only imagine what the response would be for foreign business entities, but at-least US Corporation Income Tax, Form 1120 should be disclosed. Executives have used company(s), even publicly traded companies as their piggy banks. In private situation, not only company can be a piggy bank, business Employer Identification Number (EIN) can be a proxy alternate Social Security Number for many financial activities.

Mitt Romney was sole everything for a very large number of companies. With large number of companies under sole discretion, person can do anything including manipulation of what goes into personal tax return. My point will become clear in Chapter 2 with detailed discussion specifically on this topic.

I am sure more closely someone examines, more fun items will be discovered. I would like to get back to my objective – what we can learn and use; trust me that will not only be useful, it will also be lot more fun.

Chapter 2: The Wall-Street Executive

My objective to study the tax return was to learn and indeed I learned a lot. The biggest lesson I learned is no matter who you are and what you do (even if you are unemployed or retired or a toddler), establish at-least one business entity.

Media didn't report, I learned it only by studying the tax return that Bain Capital wasn't one company. BC represents very large number of business entities. Starting from BC Inc., BC LLC, BC Venture, BC Partners, BC Partners Europe, BC Partners Asia, BC Inv, BCIP, BCIP Associates, and some of these names with numbers (such as BCIP II, BC Ptrs IV, BC Inv VII etc.).

I still have to learn the benefits of such large number of business entities, so I can't comment or suggest registering 50-100 companies; but register at-least one.

I do understand that first time (in my knowledge) Mr. John D. Rockefeller developed and employed a multi-layered structure with Standard Oil, creating a company of companies while subsidiary companies registered and operated in individual states. Since then just about every large corporation and multi-national conglomerates have used such structure – a holding company that owns multiple companies. Each subsidiary company focusing on just one thing and operates locally. If something goes wrong in any subsidiary company, other companies and the parent holding company do not suffer. The income is kept wherever it is protected. For example, most large US companies today have billions of dollars on their books in their foreign subsidiaries (according to media reports, US companies have over $1.5 Trillions offshore). IRS can't touch it because money belongs to a foreign company.

I also understand that establishing headquarters, an office consists of a telephone line and a secretary, is easy to do at a tax-free location (tax haven). Caribbean Island nations or tiny little towns of Switzerland around lakes Lucerne, Zug and Thun have plenty of examples of such International Headquarters.

My recommendation of registering a company will cost you few hundred dollars. However, I think that expense is absolutely worth it – if you want to save thousands of dollars, spend few hundred.

The Sole Proprietorship, Limited Liability Corporation (LLC), Limited Partnership (LP), S Corporation and C Corporation are few commonly used designations of a company; Mitt Romney has used every single one of them. Each designation has different tax and liability consequences.

For starter, my suggestion is that all 300 millions men, women and children (including new born babies) should establish a C Corporation. You may choose any other designation; the reason of C Corporation will become clear as you read on. According to Schedule C, Mitt Romney also has Sole Proprietorship but please avoid Sole Proprietorship. I will explain the reason why common folks should avoid it.

By registering a company, how can you amass $100 millions in IRA, I will discuss that in the next Chapter. In this chapter, I will explain how it will provide immediate cash benefits.

A number of people have also noticed that for BC entities, Mitt Romney was listed for just about every position – sole director, sole share holder, CEO etc. in 1990s. You should do the same when you register a company – instead of owner of a sole proprietary company, become sole everything of a corporation and subsequently, you do whatever you want, whenever you want it under the umbrella of a corporation.

What is a Good Designation

Sole Proprietorship is not good structure from tax point of view; it also doesn't provide any liability protection to the owner. Yes, Mitt Romney did use it; but only for (i) Director's fee from Marriott International and for fees from speeches/seminars. In fact, there is a lesson in that too – if you are getting fees and royalties, don't take it in your personal name, rather have the person pay it to a business entity. Subtract all possible expenses and pay taxes at the corporate rate.

Let's discuss sole proprietorship a bit more. There are more than 8-million sole proprietorship small businesses in the United States. As I see it, they are all sitting on a live and ticking time bomb. A single mishap can not only bankrupt the business, but also the business owner. Small business owner should not use Sole Proprietorship, it is suicidal.

Few reasons of my recommendation of C Corporation are:

1. C Corporation is an independent entity with its own tax id (employer identification number, EIN[3]). Thus, it requires a separate tax filing. But being an independent entity it is separate from the person's personal assets. Hence, if a liability or debt claim occurs against the company, business owner's personal assets are not affected.

2. The corporate tax rate is lower for C Corporation in comparison to the tax rate a person is subjected to if the equivalent income is obtained from sole proprietorship. However, when corporate income is passed to the owner such as in salary, the amount is taxed as personal income.

To avoid this and to maintain lower tax rate, don't draw salary or draw only a small salary as personal income; there are better ways to transfer

---

[3] In Mitt Romney's tax returns, all EIN numbers are blacked-out. One can make a political case that even the disclosure for 2010 is incomplete – person also needs to disclose tax returns of companies; companies for which he is sole everything.

left-over corporate income. Salary is an operating expense of the business, it is no longer income to the business and hence, business doesn't pay tax on it. By controlling the salary, owner can maintain personal income and can remain in the lower tax bracket. It should be noted that if desired, owner can transfer any/all income to himself/herself at anytime via bonus and/or dividend pay-off. But there are better ways; I will discuss it in the next sub-section.

3. If business is sold, person effectively sells stock that has been held for long time. Hence, long-term capital gain tax is applicable; a substantially lower tax-rate of 15%. On schedule D, Mitt Romney has $16,750,170 in long term capital gains, while short term capital gains are only $454,538 (taxed as ordinary income).

4. Business owner can transfer business to heirs or to other entities (such as Trust) without taxation by assigning them the officers of the

corporation or via transferring of stock at a low valuation.

I should also point-out that person should keep his/her personal finances completely separate and with proper documentation – a full paper trail. This is where Mitt Romney has excelled while many others have goofed-up and end-up in scandal.

When you are sole share holder, sole director, CEO etc., company is your piggy bank. Use it in any which way you want, nobody is stopping you and nobody is checking on you; but do it with a proper paper trail. For example, don't start writing personal checks for the business, or business checks for your house utility bills. If you write a personal check, than have it reimbursed from the business. Similarly, the initial capital the founder put-in, structure it as a loan to business with a promissory note from the company or as an investment to buy shares.

C Corporation designation also requires some formalities, i.e., meeting of the board of directors and annual shareholder meeting. When you are sole everything, these formalities can be fulfilled at any time. I doubt anybody will check, but keep a binder that maintains date and minutes of the meeting. For example, you can conduct board of directors meeting sitting on a toilet bowl! Yeah, laws and regulations are sh**.

A separate bank account, separate tax filing and certain formalities add paper work and book keeping but it provides tremendous tax advantage and personal safety.

Essentially, everyone who want to save money, should establish a company, a C Corporation, and become its sole director, sole shareholder, CEO, employee. When C Corporation issues stock, the ownership of C Corporation becomes shared. In essence, it becomes a partnership with all protections and provisions intact. With founder's own money (loan), and founder becomes an employee then effectively it becomes a partnership between founder the financier, and founder the employee and company is governed by founder the Director.

The capital structure of C Corporation is authorized number of shares and the par value of each share. This number is declared in the article of incorporation. A person can issue all shares to himself/herself and become sole shareholder. However, let me extend the Wall-Street concept and suggest leaving most shares in the company.

Leaving large number of shares in company provides additional benefits. Primary benefit being that these cannot be taken away from the person – if you don't own something, it cannot be taken away form you! Once again, if desired, you can issue (or purchase) these shares at any time – you are the sole director and CEO.

The corporation and stock buyer should also have a stock purchase agreement. To establish this purchase and the base value with the IRS, you should send a letter to the IRS. The letter maintains a record of the sale. The example language is as follows (I have extended the language of 83(b) election letters included in Mitt Romney's tax return):

א א א

Director of Internal Revenue   Date
Internal Revenue Service Center

RE: Election under Section 83(b)

This statement constitutes an election pursuant to Section 83(b) of the Internal Revenue Code of 1986, as amended from time to time.

Pursuant to Treasury Regulation Section 1.83-2, the following information is submitted:

1. Name   Address   SSN
2. Property Description: n number of share of xyz Corporation.
3. Date on which property was transferred
4. The taxable year for which election is made
5. Restriction: (Such as Corporation shall have option to repurchase)
6. Fair Market Value: (The fair market value at the time of transfer of the property with respect to which this election is made, determined without regard to any restriction other than a restriction which by its terms will never lapse, is one cent, $0.01).

7. The amount paid by the undersigned taxpayer for the property is nX$0.01
8. A copy of the statement has been furnished to xyz Corporation and the transferee of the property if different from the purchaser

Sincerely,
(Signature)

א א א

With this background, let's look at net cash benefits. In the recent years, there have been few scandals involving various Hedge Fund executives and even executives of publicly traded companies. Let me write in generalized terms, it is your piggy bank and doors open by a magical word.

Operating Expenses[4]

Operating Expenses is a truly magical word, better than Ali Baba's Open Sesame.

In the previous section, I mentioned everyone should register a business and become sole everything including CEO/President, an employee. As an employee, CEO should draw a small salary, to keep the taxes low; leaving the surplus income in the company. With minimum salary, person can control his/her personal income taxes to a lower tax bracket (with millions, Mitt Romney has 13.9%; with thousands, you can possibly get to zero).

You might be thinking that with a small salary, how would I live, person cannot buy much. Indeed, you should not buy anything from the personal income. Whatever is needed for livelihood; let the company buy it for you, its key employee! Let's look at what I have learned:

---

[4] This discussion explains my comment at the end of Chapter 1.

Consider lunch/dinner, if business can afford it, CEO can eat at any restaurant no matter how expensive and order any Italian or French wine. Have a meeting with someone and it is a business meeting paid by the company. For company, it is an operating expense. Keep the receipt in case IRS wants to audit (they like to audit common people like you and me).

Consider lunch with your friend CEO to discuss business strategies or future dealings – *selection of restaurant for lunch on next Friday*. Of-course, one meeting is not enough. The friend CEO will pick the tab of the second meeting and have it reimbursed as a business expense from his/her company. Am I forgetting IRS per diem regulation; no, that is designed for the poor sole-proprietors to encourage eating hamburgers and to keep them healthy.

Ever wondered how a real estate agent, who hardly makes any sale, drives around in a Mercedes? Or ever felt tired of paying for auto insurance. Forget about puny insurance, company can buy or lease a new car for the use of its employees. This is what I was wondering in the last chapter – no car licensing fee.

Mercedes and BMWs are for the common folks, think-of Rolls or Austin Martin. When company's key employee, the CEO, goes somewhere, it should provide a good image of the company. Now, you don't own a car, you don't pay for the insurance. Its company's car, company will pay for its insurance, just as it will pay for the gasoline; all operating expenses. Don't bother with $0.25/mile tax deduction; you can't find any such thing in Mitt Romney's return; such non-sense only shows-up in the tax return of common people.

While at-it, don't feel envious of other CEOs. If company can afford it, company can buy a Learjet or Gulfstream for its employees. Of-course, CEO's time is more important, so most of the time it will be busy flying CEO than anyone else (don't rub it in the faces of law-makers – CEO of GM lost his job).

Ever worried about home mortgage? Don't own a home personally – no home, no mortgage. Company has surplus cash that needs to be invested. Real estate is pretty good investment – company should buy a mansion with swimming pool, tennis court and servant quarters (company has to hire someone for up keeping of its investment; this will be your household help). Keeping an empty house is not a good idea, so company should rent it out. Wait, doesn't that self-proprietary Company, we were talking about needs a place. The rent is of-course an operating expense of the self-proprietary company. Don't get too excited, but if company can afford it, company can also get an apartment on the Fifth Avenue in Manhattan overlooking the Central Park because our CEO has lunch-meetings with the Wall-Street investors on regular basis. And to decorate this apartment, company needs to buy couple of original Monet and Picasso.

Its middle of February, everyone is fed-up with snow. Isn't a conference being held in George Town,

Cayman Islands on …; oh, does it matter on what. Company would want to send its CEO to check what the conference is all about or may be just to set-up a subsidiary company. If company has not purchased a jet (yet), CEO would need a chartered plane. Family just tags along on an empty plane, just as they crashed in the CEO's suite at the Ritz.

Wife or Girl friend wants a new dress. Company can hire her and provide a necklace (diamonds) along with the dress for …. Well, consultant to improve the moral of executive may be too much for some readers; how about model for the advertising campaign. Just make sure her picture appears somewhere, such as on an obscure section of the company's web-site in case IRS started to get tipsy with us mortals. By the way, did I mention that our CEO can also appear in the ad in a three-piece Armani suit personalized tailored in Milan, paid by the company.

Birthday of spouse, have a Roman party on Las Vegas strip; just invite few employees and it is off-site meeting to determine strategic direction of the company. Even federal agencies hold such meetings; everything operating expenses.

Don't forget, operating expenses are pre-tax dollars; that is a considerable cash advantage.

Transfer everything to company, don't convert business profits into higher salary or personal income – if there is no personal income, there are no personal taxes. Take $1.00 in annual salary and establish yourself as an altruist. A number of CEOs of large companies have done that. It's a very good PR. The real money resides with shares that are collected as stock option or flat-out stock grant.

With $1.00 annual salary you can forget taxes; in-fact, if you wish, you can apply for food stamps. Car, home, airplane, yacht are all company assets for its employees, CEO is just an employee. Lunch, dinner, trips (don't use the word "vacation") are all necessary business expenses. Who said to conduct work-meeting over a Subway sandwich. Company has surplus cash, why not eat at the Four Seasons and while waiting for the table, take a bottle of '63 Don Perignon with Beluga caviar – it may taste like horse sh** (manure), but we are not talking taste here.

I hope readers got the point. There is nothing illegal here, it's a private company and its sole director can choose how company is run, spend or invest its income. Because details are "confidential", nobody can question where exactly money is going; it is an expense, IRS can't do a thing. Your personal tax return also becomes clean – many of your expenses go away, so you don't need to take puny deductions; you can focus on big deductions.

I only mentioned expenses and day-to-day life; over the years, media has reported a number of cases when person's life remained unaffected even when person has accrued large personal debt or when person has lost big personal liability suit. Transfer everything to an entity, a Trust and become its trustee. Don't own anything and go broke on paper.

If person is broke, creditor cannot collect anything. Being an independent entity, Trust, on the other hand can spend anything, anytime, in any manner according to the direction of trustee without being affected by the claimant. If questions are asked on money or holding of trust, you can even claim ignorance and deflect all questions – responsibility is of trustee.

Back to the surplus income our CEO will leave in the company, it can be transferred to the person via a number of methods such as dividend (tax rate 15%), retirement contribution and other deferred compensation mechanisms. In the next chapter, I will discuss it in detail.

Earlier, I mentioned that the business can be passed-on to heirs without taxation. With C Corporation, this transfer is simply to assign heirs as the officer of the corporation, i.e., son/daughter can become the next CEO and director. Founder CEO was an employee, he is retiring. Corporation hires a new CEO; it just happens that the new CEO is the son/daughter of the old CEO. As company has majority of shares with voting rights limited to the founder/CEO, founder/CEO doesn't pass-on large number of shares or estate to his/her heirs. Nonetheless, when heir becomes the CEO, he/she gets the voting rights and full control. He/she can run the company in any which way desired. Any time in future, if they want, they can issue these shares to themselves (a purchase at valuation decided by them).

If no estate is passed-on, there are no taxes. Who cares about "death taxes"; let congress tinker any which way they want.

While mentioning death, we also want to protect the family of our CEO. From the surplus that was left in the company by not taking large salary, company can buy life insurance for the CEO; another operating expense. Because our CEO is very important person, company can buy few million dollars policy. If something happens to our CEO, beneficiary gets the policy's amount without taxation.

Let's consider one more example before moving to the next chapter.

Above, I mentioned that our CEO should leave a large number of shares in the company for future use. But let's say our CEO wants to sell the company and 51% shares are in his/her name. One possibility is that our CEO value the whole company to his/her 51% shares and sell, thus, get the total value. But if planned ahead, our CEO can buy leftover 49% shares at a much higher price. It is a non-public company, investor and company can "negotiate" any price. Our CEO continues to run the company for one year or leave the company but remains its CEO on paper. During this year, company can contribute its cash (including the cash from the stock sale) in dividend payments and to the retirement of our CEO. All money from company's account is gone, company is almost bankrupt. Then the sale occurs, 100% shares owned by the CEO with very little value, 49% shares were held over a year; hence, person will be subjected to large long-term capital loss. The original 51% share might create some capital gain (par value was very small when company was registered). But the 49% shares can cause a significant long-term capital loss. In fact, the sale of shares can be adjusted to cause net long-term as well as short-term capital loss; offsetting gains and income from other sources.

Now, you understand why in the beginning of the book, I mentioned an unprecedented and great learning opportunity.

Common folks like me can't go overseas to Caribbean Island nations or European nations like Switzerland, probably we don't need to – there is plenty of Swiss cheese right here, made in Washington D.C.

Chapter 3: How to Get $100 Millions In IRA

Now that all expenses are taken care-of, let's think of retirement – we do want to retire rich.

So, let's get back to $100M IRA that is giving headache to many pundits. I think that the reason they are scratching their head is because they are looking only at the personal contribution limit. They need to abandon the book knowledge; book knowledge doesn't work, they need to get street smart, Wall-Street that is.

Indeed, personal contributions over a period of 15-years would most likely not yield $100M; few millions may be. Readers should note that all investments of Mitt Romney were not successful. Even in 2010, he had carryover long-term loss of

$4,844,089. In retirement account as well, he would have ups and downs, not just straight line up.

So, how did he do it? The primary difficulty I have is limiting the imagination to personal contributions. Who said money in IRA came only by personal contributions – a corporation can contribute anything into an employee retirement account such as 401K, there is no limit, no restrictions.

An explanation could be as simple as $100M (or whatever the amount is) contributed by Bain Capital while he was there. When he left, he rolled his 401K into an IRA; nothing wrong, nothing illegal.

He was sole everything of very large number of companies. If these companies have contributed just one million dollars each, IRA would become in tens of millions of dollars, if not hundred.[5]

---

[5] It is certainly a benefit but I doubt this was the primary reason of creating such large number of companies.

Executives of large companies and Wall-Street executives get millions of dollars of contribution into their retirement account when they leave (sometimes even when they are continuing). Bonuses and Severance packages worth tens of millions of dollars often include a large portion that goes into retirement account. It is a standard practice – why pay taxes when you can defer it.

At Advantest America Corporation, I myself received extra year-end bonus directly contributed into my 401K; this was in-addition to the normal company's matching contribution that most employers provide.

Most companies don't do such things for employees. The bad aspect is that most people don't even know and hence, don't ask to deposit severance or bonus payment into retirement. We don't ask, they don't tell. This is exactly why we need to examine and learn.

Although, it is a very straightforward and simple explanation, looking into, extrapolating numbers and little imagination, I think of a different scenario.

My speculative scenario is that in the early days of Bain Capital, for example in 1995-96, IRA owned some initial shares. It could be done by investing some of the existing IRA money into Bain Capital or simply as a founder's ownership. The par value of these shares could easily be fraction of a penny.

It is also likely that in later years, some IRA money was invested into some of the companies that were bought-and-sold by Bain Capital. These investments also resulted into good gains.

When he left, Bain Capital made a large contribution in his retirement account and IRA ownership was sold back to Bain Capital.

One of the consideration behind this reasoning is that Bain Capital earned tremendous money and than almost abruptly went bankrupt while there was no "financial crises" or "credit crunch". We don't know the reason why Bain Capital went bankrupt, I am only speculating.

Readers should also note that transactions in my scenario are not illegal and a sole director/CEO can easily conduct them.

Political embarrassment today is an entirely different issue. Even in 2005, did he know he will run for the President?

Contribution into 401K is the simplest process. It is an employee benefit, an operating expense to the company; company doesn't pay taxes on an expense. But because it is a deferred income, receiver doesn't pay taxes either.

Better Than $100 Millions In IRA

Although, nobody knows the exact amount or even a close number for Mitt Romney's IRA; whatever it is, it is large, in tens of millions of dollars. But there is a problem, at-least this is what everyone thinks – he will have to pay taxes when he will start withdrawing. Even the amount of minimum distributions will be quite large.

Will Mitt Romney pay large percentage of his IRA withdrawals in taxes? I doubt it; master always keeps couple of tricks in his sleeve.

As I have learned a number of things from just one year of tax return, I won't bet that he has this problem; pundit shouldn't bet too. He very well may have a solution that he will use when needed. There is no need for him to talk now. Forget IRA, he is not talking his finances at-all right now regardless of the political pressure.

So, let's imagine a bit what can or cannot be done with our puny knowledge.

Question: Is there anything better than $100 millions in IRA?

Certainly.

$100 millions in Roth IRA.

Money in Roth IRA is tax exempt; there are no minimum distribution requirements for Roth IRA either. Why follow forced regulation of IRA and pay taxes on withdrawals when a structure, free of regulations and taxes is possible.

We often blame congress for not doing anything useful – they created Roth IRA. It's a free ride to become a millionaire. If you don't use it, it's your fault, don't curse congress.

Remember our CEO in chapter 2; let's consider he/she is a 60 year old person. Close to retirement and hence, according to the conventional wisdom not a good candidate for Roth IRA. But let's say our CEO does set-up a Roth IRA and fund it from his small salary. On this Roth IRA, our CEO declares his/her 2-years old grand child as beneficiary. Now, the whole amount of Roth IRA is transferred to this grand child (heir), after his/her demise. The distribution time-frame is also now according to the kid's life expectancy, allowing the amount to continually grow without taxation. Whether our CEO is a millionaire or not, the grand kid definitely will be and the kid won't pay any taxes on this amount either.

Some readers might be saying – cut the crap, we want $100 millions.

Whatever is known, Mitt Romney doesn't have $100M in Roth IRA; if he did, America would have been asking Warren Buffet to move over. He has money in simple IRA; he has not use Roth structure so far.

Question: Can you get $100M in Roth IRA?

Certainly!

How?

Well, the same way you get $100M in IRA.

I am not kidding.

Let me back-track a little. My scenario is for our CEO of chapter 2; or may be for you, who have yet to register a company.

In simple terms – establish a Roth IRA; register a company; invest some of Roth IRA money (let's say $100) in the company – for example, purchase shares at $0.0001. When company becomes profitable and has $100M, sell Roth IRA shares back to the company – forget $100M, you can get Billions in Roth IRA if company has that much money.

Remember that 83(b) election letter to the IRS; don't forget to send that letter when Roth IRA buys stock. If you become lazy and forgetful, you will remain a commoner.

The "sale" would result into immense capital gain; but, it's Roth IRA, all gains are tax exempt, money is yours to enjoy.

Now, readers might have started to see the benefit of registering a company regardless of what they do or whatever is the age. $100M may not be possible for everyone, but why not do it with thousands. This is very straightforward, no puzzle to solve in any step.

Of-course, in future, Wall-Streeters can and most likely will do it with millions and billions. But first, they need to find a solution for step 1 – how to open Roth IRA. Is that a complex enough problem for them to figure it out? This was the major dilemma I had, what I wrote in Preface. It is a risk I took, let's see how it works out – if they figure it out before the hole is plugged, Uncle Sam will really be pissed-off with me.

But Mitt Romney already has money in IRA, can he transfer it into Roth IRA?

Yes of-course. But our pundits will tell that it would be a taxable event. Some real illustrious pundits may even say that he is not eligible for Roth IRA.

Let me leave it for Wall-Streeters and pundits to figure out step 1.

I think the main question readers probably want to ask: Can he transfer money from his IRA into a Roth IRA without paying taxes?

Answer is surprisingly, yes.

I am not going to write that scenario in this book. Besides, I am learning from him; he doesn't need to learn anything from me and of-course, I don't want to educate Wall-Streeters.

A Second Tax Free IRA

Roth IRA came into existence in 1997. What was the tax exempt mechanism before that? Where were rich people stashing money tax free?

I am referring to non-profit structure – foundations, charitable entities. Government recognizes non-profit foundations as charitable organizations. IRS considers private foundations as nonexempt charitable entities but for all practical purposes their tax obligation is very little. IRS also gives tax exempt status if an entity fulfills certain criteria; that list is also an eye-opener.

Our objective is to eliminate taxes for our money; non-profit umbrella does that by definition. Money in a private foundation, charity needs not to be spent; it can be set aside for some charitable purpose (for you) in future. There is a requirement to provide grants for a certain portion. But once again, Washington produces so much Swiss cheese, in last 2-years since I start looking finances/taxes, I have often wondered if the name of the country should be changed.

Just about every rich person I have looked at has a Non-profit Foundation or Charitable Trust. Money given to such personal foundations and charities is recognized as charitable gift and person is allowed to take deduction, reducing person's taxable income and taxes.

The problem is, if a person or for-profit corporation gives money to someone else's charity, giver can take a tax deduction but that money is gone.

On the other hand, consider if it is your own Charity/Foundation. In such a case, you not only get the tax deduction on "charitable gift", money still remains under your control.

In 2010, Mitt Romney gave $1,458,807 to Tyler Charitable Foundation. All of it was deducted as gift to charity, reducing taxable income by this amount and subsequently, huge reduction in taxes. The beauty is that whole amount remained under his control unrestricted. According to 2010 return, Form 990-PF, Tyler Foundation had assets worth more than $10 millions.

Although I think he will not, but for example, if he wants he can pay that money to himself – personal trusts and foundations are allowed to pay salaries to officers, directors, trustees, employees etc.; there is no restriction. He can also keep it under Tyler Foundation as long as he wants, money remains protected, no taxes, no nothing. There is nothing wrong in it, nothing illegal.

Think about these personal charities and foundations for a minute – it is a much better tax deferral mechanism than your IRA. Consider a 50-year old man wants to help his young son/daughter in buying a home, car or setting a boutique shop. Person has money in his IRA, but taking it out would not only trigger taxes but also penalty for early withdrawal. If the same person has money under a non-profit umbrella (charitable trust or foundation), he can designate his son/daughter as an officer/director/trustee/employee of the charity/foundation and simply pay whatever is needed as salary. For son/daughter, it will be personal income and they will be required to pay taxes.

Surprisingly, non-profit umbrella even provides a solution for the taxes of son/daughter; son/daughter needs not to pay taxes either. If it is house or car, non-profit can simply buy it for the use of officer/director/employee – remember the operating expenses, I discussed in chapter 2. If car is needed, give a car allowance; if house is needed, give house allowance. Even respected charities and universities give such allowances to their executives. In case of a business such as a boutique shop, non-profit can simply "invest". No early withdrawal, no penalty, no taxes.

Forget son/daughter, you can use any and all assets in non-profit charity/foundation for your own purpose, there is no real restriction.

Non-profit charity/foundation is much better than simple IRA, may be not quite good as Roth IRA. But then, some people have made it better than Roth IRA.

What I have written above is very well known and has been in practice for long time. Without naming names, some people have used charity/foundation to generate revenue (public donations), revenue that was used for their own purposes – Roth IRA can't generate such income for you.

Everyone may not have $10 millions, but there is no reason why you cannot stash away few thousand dollars, and while doing it reduce your present taxes. The tax return form will be different; for less than $50,000, it is Form 990-N; but in most cases, 990-EZ is what you will need.

Transfer money from taxable entity or from your name to non-profit entity and use it any which way you want, whenever you want it. It is your second IRA, with no restriction on withdrawal and no minimum distribution requirements.

Chapter 4: Tinker Tyler Solider Sailor

In 1974, David Cornwell, a former member of the British foreign service wrote a brilliant detective novel under pseudonym John Le Carre. Many readers might have read and possibly also seen the movie. I might have made a mistake in the title of this chapter, but readers can check it out. The background of the novel is the problem British counter intelligence service faced – how to identify Soviet agents and double agents living in England under false pretence. The old British sleuth George Smiley in the British counter intelligence noticed a single discrepancy. Detailed examination led to the identity of bad guys and trail stretched showing exactly how and what Soviet intelligence chief has done.

In last two years, I have learned that when it comes to finances and money, reality is very different than what is on the surface. Even the Olympics Gold medal is not gold, it's 90% silver. The reason has been given as cost, even when it goes to athletes, primary actors in the main events – the games; the 47 events in London Olympics. The wining and dining of various committee members, their enormous compensations and benefits are all hidden from the view; no one question that cost or asks to curb it.

In recent years, I have noticed some discrepancies in various things and places, even at very respected organizations; or at-least I thought they were discrepancies. Remember, I am in the learning phase – learn what is possible and how it can be done. So, when I see a discrepancy (or I think so), I try to get details; and indeed details give very interesting and eye opening pictures.

I have been discussing taxes; individual personal taxes and taxes of corporations. Whole discussion in the last chapter, IRA vs Roth IRA is basically to defer taxes or possibly have the money tax exempt.

In chapter 2, I suggested registering a company; wouldn't it be good if the company itself is tax exempt. Well, Government has already created such structure for us to use, why not use what is available, many rich people do. Yes, I am referring to non-profit structure that I discussed a little bit in the last chapter.

Let's look at an example; it will help you to understand how screwed-up my mind is.

A Respected Charity

Red Cross is possibly the most recognized charitable organization in the world. As information is public, it is easy for me to use it as an example. There is one another reason, I am choosing this as an example; I will explain that reason later.

In the tax filing of American Red Cross, Form 990, part III, the mission is listed as, "The American National Red Cross, a humanitarian organization led by volunteers and guided by its congressional charter and the fundamental principle of the International Red Cross movement, will provide relief to victims of disaster and help people prevent, prepare for, and respond to emergencies."

Let's start with grants and assistance Red Cross provided. In 2010[6] tax filing, Red Cross listed a total of $81,749,998 for grants and assistance to individuals in the United States (Part IX, the Statement of Functional Expenses, line 2); and $300,552,000 for grants and assistance to governments, organizations and individuals outside the United States (Part IX, line 3).

On schedule F, the grants and assistance to organizations outside the United States is disclosed. For the year 2010, Red Cross listed 74 grants, given for disaster preparedness, disaster recovery, disaster response and general health. These recipient organizations being recognized charities in the

---

[6] I hope readers will appreciate my choice of 2010 tax return.

foreign countries and recognized as tax exempt by the IRS.

The list is given in table 1. The sum of grants listed in Table 1 is $280,760,855.

Table 1: Grants and other assistance to organizations or entities outside the United States. From Red Cross 2010 tax filing, Schedule F, form 990.

Cent Am/Caribbean	$25,086	Cent Am/Caribbean	$5,295,025
E. Asia/Pacific	$561,655	Cent Am/Caribbean	$1,285,000
Europe/Iceland/Greenland	$125,840	Cent Am/Caribbean	$500,000
Cent Am/Caribbean	$120,008	Cent Am/Caribbean	$191,772
E. Asia/Pacific	$206,000,000	Cent Am/Caribbean	$136,400
Mid East/N. Africa	$14,284	Cent Am/Caribbean	$2,985,834
Russia	$172,677	Cent Am/Caribbean	$1,196,818
Sub-Sahara Africa	$367,738	Cent Am/Caribbean	$1,318,993
Russia	$31,680	Cent Am/Caribbean	$1,049,094
Sub-Sahara Africa	$100,104	Cent Am/Caribbean	$116,721
S. Asia	$9,040	Cent Am/Caribbean	$3,821,078
Sub-Sahara Africa	$101,176	S. Asia	$110,427
North America	$507,190	Cent Am/Caribbean	$279,663
S. Asia	$49,921	South America	$187,073
E. Asia/Pacific	$772,000	Russia	$701,069
Cent Am/Caribbean	$35,221	Cent Am/Caribbean	$133,376
Europe/Iceland/Greenland	$7,937,083	Sub-Sahara Africa	$100,307
Europe/Iceland/Greenland	$2,464,256	S. Asia	$986,331
Russia	$49,700	Russia	$21,374
Cent Am/Caribbean	$252,557	Sub-Sahara Africa	$646,637
Russia	$49,442	E. Asia/Pacific	$195,094
Cent Am/Caribbean	$80,000	Russia	$17,477

South America	$91,000	Sub-Sahara Africa	$129,778
South America	$93,506	Russia	$362,789
E. Asia/Pacific	$2,049,903	E. Asia/Pacific	$195,565
South America	$461,053	Cent Am/Caribbean	$3,312,029
Cent Am/Caribbean	$364,151	Cent Am/Caribbean	$2,686,164
South America	$79,470	Cent Am/Caribbean	$6,257,770
Cent Am/Caribbean	$102,895	Cent Am/Caribbean	$928,638
Cent Am/Caribbean	$32,187	Cent Am/Caribbean	$1,826,488
South America	$93,576	Cent Am/Caribbean	$1,376,876
Cent Am/Caribbean	$3,186,416	Cent Am/Caribbean	$144,746
Cent Am/Caribbean	$1,669,632	Cent Am/Caribbean	$1,500,200
Cent Am/Caribbean	$5,763,295	Cent Am/Caribbean	$61,001
Cent Am/Caribbean	$5,238,387	Cent Am/Caribbean	$273,317
E. Asia/Pacific	$899,937	Cent Am/Caribbean	$149,802
S. Asia	$220,348	Cent Am/Caribbean	$107,715

In this list, the recipients of 37 grants are Central America/Caribbean; the total amount is $53,804,355. Although, the word Haiti is not listed but it is fair to assume that the majority of these grants were for the Haiti disaster.

Now, let's also look at the total revenue and expenses, this is Part I of Form 990. Line 12 specifies total revenue as $3,452,960,387 (let's call it $3.45B); line 18 specifies total expenses as $3,422,010,386 (let's call it $3.42B). The detailed breakdown of expenses is given in Part IX, the Statement of Functional Expenses. I will get to that in a minute. Let me just complete the Part I of form 990.

The line 13 is grants and similar amounts (combined US and non-US), it is $382,301,998; line 17, other expenses are $1,345,550,396; line 15 is salaries, other compensation, employee benefits, it is $1,694,157,992 (let's call it $1.69B).

Now, readers might be getting the idea, where I am going with all this – yes, 49% of the total revenue ($1.69B out of $3.45B) went directly to employees. Other expenses (I would like to use the term operating expenses), are almost 39% of the total revenue (almost $1.35B out of $3.45B). The amount of grants for the victims, the primary objective of the charity is only about $382M, 11% of the total revenue – dime on a dollar!

Is it that bad? Please remember that this is the good charity. It is the Red Cross; not a charity of some individual rich person or celebrity. Whenever a disaster strikes, middle class Americans open their heart and give freely. In future, please check who you are giving to, to the victims or to the employees/executives of the charity.

In Part IX, line 8 is pension plan contribution, the amount itself is $92,008,268 - $92M for the pension of employees, while the sum of 37 grants to Central America/Caribbean (assuming it is Haiti) is $53.8M. Under liabilities, pension and post retirement is listed as $672,134,249; this is where your future donations will go.

In the same section, Part IX, line 9 is other employee benefits, that amount is $164,989,964; and line 11g, fees for other non-employee services is $169,502,436. Forget salary/wages and pension of the employees, the "other" (employee and non-employee), itself is $334,492,400, 120% of all grants listed in table 1.

Not to be confused, I did mention earlier the amount listed on line 2 and line 3 of part IX; that totals to $382,301,998. Interested readers should check, the tax filing as well as audited financial statements is available on the website.

The breakdown of Functional Expenses includes travel, legal, management, office expenses, equipment purchase etc. that one can understand. The other expenses are for you to decipher – I did mention in chapter 2 that operating expenses is a magical word.

About half of the grants in Table 1 are of less than $250,000. Schedule J lists a number of employees; every one of them has compensation of more than $300,000. The number of individuals who received over $100,000 is given as 1078.

When you look into charity of individual rich people and celebrities, what can you expect? You can't get explanation of other expenses from the Red Cross; when it is some individual's charity, will you get an explanation? The tax form for private foundations is Form 990PF. IRS collect these forms but can't do a thing; IRS cannot dictate how much is being spend and where.

Now, you understand why I took your time entertaining operating expenses in chapter 2. Non-profit organizations are no different. For-profit-corporation most likely will get a bad-rep because of a million dollar party. Non-profit organizations hold 2-million dollars or 3-million dollars party; they call it charity ball and in-fact get praise. Charity is indeed a very good business.

Have I got distracted?

My home address is 990; it is there, all hell breaks loose for me.

Chapter 5: Lessons Learned

Work hard, do your job is conventional wisdom; pretty stupid, if you ask me. Ditch conventional wisdom, it doesn't work. All moves and their counter moves are known; besides the game is rigged. You need to use either unconventional moves or the moves masters use.

I have mentioned that I live in California. Cities, Counties are going bankrupt, probably State will too. I am thinking to move out.

When we can pay less than 15% to the Federal government, does CA think we are stupid and pay 10% in state taxes?

If any state takes away your money in state taxes, there is no need to live there. Certainly, there is no need to live in the states like California and New

York that take almost 10%; not a single person should be living there. Move out. Move to a state that has no state taxes like Nevada, Texas, Wyoming, Florida, Alaska etc. Most Billionaires call such states their home. Every time, Forbes list come out, local news papers and TV stations proudly announce how many Billionaire "call" such and such city their home. The only exception may be Warren Buffet. He lives in Omaha, what does he know? He even wants to tax the rich. There is only one word to describe him – reasonable. You want to play a rigged game, don't be reasonable; law makers don't listen to reasonable people.

Moving out doesn't mean selling your home, putting your furniture and other personal belongings in a truck and go. Take a short vacation. Go to Vegas, have a drink and play some poker (you'll learn not to flinch with my ideas); go to Miami and swim in the ocean (water in San Francisco is too cold); go to Orlando and visit Disney parks (objective is serious, no goofing around); go to Huston and enjoy warm waters of the gulf (Huston will not have any problem); go to Yellow Stone, a bear might walk in front of you (watch bare necessities of your life); go to Alaska and see glaciers disappearing (who knows, you might also see Russia); go to any such place that fancy you. The only constraint – it should be in a state that has no taxes.

While enjoying your vacation, rent a place, possibly a studio apartment. There are plenty of low rent studio apartments available everywhere, it doesn't matter if there are 10 members in your family – you are not going to live there; you are going to "call" it your home. Another possibility is to rent a room with a local resident; with room in a house, you don't need to worry about break-in in the empty studio apartment.

Declare the address of this rental unit your residence. You will require to change your driver's license and car registration, but that is about it. Now, you don't need to pay taxes of your previous state.

For example, if you are a resident of California, drive to Las Vegas or Reno, whichever is easier; rent a room/apartment (plenty are available for around $200/month; some even give free rent for the first month); change your driver's license and the registration of your car; put this address on all your business dealings (income should be at this address); you are set – your California taxes are gone.

The Most Important Lesson

Now, you are in a new tax-free state, establish a company. The biggest lesson I learned is no matter who you are, how old you are, what you do, establish at-least one corporation. If you don't have a corporation, you are on your own, eat hamburgers, munch potato chips in front of the TV and curse everyone around you.

Similar to a for profit corporation, you also need to establish a non-profit Charity/Foundation.

Everybody should have a for-profit and a non-profit entity. This lesson alone more than justify my time reading tax returns and spend time writing these 100-pages. Most rich people already have such duo-structure; if only few middle class American register a for-profit and a non-profit, I will consider every second of my time well spent.

Two are Better Than One

There are multiple benefits of establishing both a for-profit and a non-profit corporation. The primary benefit is that it allows more revenue streams. A for-profit corporation has to provide goods/services to get public money, but non-profit corporation can get grants, money that is free and clear.

The duo-structure also allows spreading money and stashing it in more ways that are not possible by using only taxable or only tax-exempt umbrella and drawing benefits in more ways. And the best of all, it leaves Uncle Sam to hang and dry-out in more ways.

With both for-profit and non-profit structures, you get an amazing tax deferral mechanism – you can defer any income for any duration just by shifting money into charity umbrella, gift to non-profit foundation/charity.

I mentioned source of revenue – public money, government grants. Philanthropy is such a good career that depending upon what business you are in, you may indeed get state and the federal funding. Most rich people, whenever they get a chance, also conduct a fund raising event for their charity and collect donations from individuals. Federal and state funding is dependent upon lobbying.

IRS recognizes lobbying as functional expenses (operating expenses) – IRS doesn't make laws, congress does; members of congress get campaign contributions from lobbyists. Give campaign contributions to get grants, a fair trade; it is business after-all.

In the nation's history, there are very few incidents when the governor of a state was recalled; California is one of them. State had and still has billions in deficit, but it was funding hundreds of reports that have nothing to do with anything. California requiring annual report on the kangaroo population in Australia is just one example – so that money can hop-around. You probably have heard such examples from every state and federal offices. In 2012, Jerry Brown found more than 50 such projects, buried in long obscure documents that nobody reads; most likely many are still hiding. How well you can bury government funding of your charity again depends upon your lobbying effort.

Be Kind and Generous to the World

We are the kindest people human race has ever seen. We want to help not only every poor and mal-nourished kid around the world, but also animals and even insects in the far-away lands! Establish a non-profit charity and get government grant. Team-up with a professor, it will be worth while in generating proposals and PR will be great.

As a director/trustee/employee of the non-profit, you can draw your salary (don't draw a large salary, it would be recognized as personal income), non-profit corporation will of-course pay all "operating expenses". Whatever is earned, whether it is donation, grant money or business income, it is within the non-profit umbrella. In the context of C Corporation, I suggested to leave surplus income in the company; do the same under non-profit umbrella. Money may not be in your name, but still remains in your control. For any reason if you decide to transfer it in your name, you can certainly do that.

Once you set-up a Charity, advertise it. Go online, show couple of pictures of starving children or dying cats/dogs, it is likely that you will get enough donations to support all kinds of "operating expenses".

Consider charity for the poor aborigine tribal children on Juan Fernandez Islands in the South Pacific. Don't question me if there is such a tribe. Didn't you read Robinson Crusoe; these children are his descendent. When documents are notarized, stamped and sealed by the government officials, the tribe exists.

But if you don't like my tribe, pick your own; visit them, give them $1.00 per person and take their signatures/thumb-prints. Also take some pictures and certificate from their leader as a precaution. I doubt it but IRS might ask; journalists are dangerous, they may poke questions. African nations are very popular to find poor people, tribes, animals and insects that need help. Being born in India; India, Bangladesh, Bhutan and Nepal are my favorite nations. Cost used to be $1-$2, with inflation, now it will cost about $10, but you can get official certificate with government seal and glorified letters about your good charity. These are not counterfeit; these are real, signed by the real government officials and stamped with real government seal. Be careful, use local currency and you should never flash money; if you flash money, price will go up rapidly.

At-home, because of your kind nature, now, you will be rewarded with additional tax exemptions and deductions.

I am not kidding – celebrities, rich-and-famous do it routinely; you can too, you should too. All you need to do is to get clear in your own mind and set-up your personal charitable foundation.

Now, the finesse; I did mention, if we learn, we may even be able to extend the existing practices:

When you have your own charity, you may want to add an extra layer of protection and become bullet-proof against IRS or anyone else like those dangerous journalists; or just in case, laws and regulations are changed.

As an added security, setup one more charity trust/foundation. But set it up offshore, in warm Turquoise waters of Caribbean. Now, your US charity can give grants to this offshore foundation that is also recognized as charitable entity by the IRS. Nobody can demand any kind of explanation from foreign entity; if they do, tell them to go to hell, we are doing charity here. Any number of grants and any amount the foreign charity receive, it can spend in any way it desires without disclosing anything to anyone in the US – it is its business. It can give all of it to a person, you, the director/trustee/employee, no one can question. IRS can only question US charity; US charity is giving to offshore charity, what happens after that is none of IRS business.

The best part is, I think Congress can't change these laws; they can't even touch these laws. Laws and regulation governing non-profit organizations are off-limit, no one can touch them.

Just about every rich and influential person in the nation is affiliated with a non-profit; this itself is a reason, good enough to establish a non-profit entity and ride the same ride.

Non-profits cover all schools and universities, churches, temples, synagogues and mosques, various political organizations and numerous private foundations and charitable trusts; even the list of non-profits that IRS recognizes as "exempt" is very extensive. Interested reader should look at the list in the instruction of Form 990, and while at-it, also look at the allowable "functional expenses".

Don't you see, Saints do charity; Saints have divine powers, magical things happen with the Divine Power!　　　□ □ □

Other business book from the author

In Your Face IRS: Zero Taxes

I am not talking here how mega companies shift their revenue to off-shore tax havens. I am also not talking here how billionaires pay hardly 14%-15% of their income in taxes (14%-15% is too much for me). I am talking here how middle class America can pay zero taxes. If you are a farmer/rancher, mom-and-pop store owner, contractor, doctor/lawyer/accountant providing services, small business owner, you should not pay a dime in taxes.

Students don't even have any earning, may be $8-$10 an hour earning from a burger place; taxes are not really an issue for them yet, but ballooning unforgivable student loan is. What I am talking here is that they need not to pay it back.

No, don't hide your income; don't break any laws. I am in-fact suggesting to follow the law to the letter. IRS can't do a sh**. IRS doesn't make laws, they follow laws. Congress makes laws. After reading this book, will congress change laws I am referring to? I challenge them, no, I dare them. If members of the congress even think to touch these laws, they will shoot in their own foot; their own assets will become venerable.

.

Individual's act is small but it validates a hypothesis. Once we have proof-of-concept, we can repeat it – basic scientific principle. I would like to see that all middle class Americans eliminate their taxes.

Paperback ISBN 978-1477640456
Kindle Version ISBN 978-0985737009

Rochit Rajsuman

A cool Silicon Valley nerd, Rochit Rajsuman received Ph. D. in Electrical Engineering from Colorado State University. He has worked both in the academia and industry in engineering and engineering management positions. In academic career, Dr. Rajsuman has served as Assistant Professor in Computer Engineering and Science Department at Case Western Reserve University and as Pinson Chair Professor in the Electrical Engineering Department at San Jose State University. In industrial career, he has worked at Silicon Valley semiconductor companies LSI Logic and Equator Technologies and as manager of research at Advantest America R&D Center and as Chief Scientist at Advantest America Corporation. He has also founded two technology companies.

Dr. Rajsuman has authored a number of books including three computer/electrical engineering books, published by the Artech House Inc., a division of Horizon House. He has written numerous papers and 30 awarded US patents related to design and testing of semiconductor integrated circuits.